Jellyfish

Victoria Blakemore

Table of Contents

What Are Jellyfish?

Jellyfish are marine animals. They are related to sea anemones. They are known for their round shape and stinging tentacles.

Jellyfish get their name from the kind of body they have. It is soft and jelly-like.

Kinds of Jellyfish

There are about 200

different kinds of jellyfish.

They differ in size, color,

shape, and where they live.

Jellyfish range in size from

about one centimeter long

to over fifty feet long.

The Lion's mane jellyfish is the

biggest kind of jellyfish.

Jellyfish do not have a solid skeleton like other animals. They are mostly made up of water. This is why they change shape as they move.

The round area on top of the jellyfish is called the bell or hood. It provides **structure** for the jellyfish.

The bell keeps all of the jellyfish's

insides together. It contains parts

like the stomach.

Jellyfish do not have a brain or lungs. They get oxygen through their skin. The nerves on their tentacles help them feel prey.

Tentacles are the part of the jellyfish that can sting. They can be short or long. The Lion's mane jellyfish has tentacles that can be over fifty feet long!

Jellyfish have a mouth. It is in the middle of their body, under the bell. Their tentacles surround the mouth.

Habitat

Jellyfish are mainly **marine** animals, which means that they are usually found in saltwater.

There are a few kinds of jellyfish that can live in freshwater.

Range

Jellyfish are found in every ocean on Earth.

Some jellyfish are found close to the surface. Others are only found deep in the ocean.

Jellyfish are **carnivores**, which means that they eat meat. Their diet is made up of small fish, shrimp, and plankton.

Larger kinds of jellyfish may sometimes eat other jellyfish.

Small jellyfish are sometimes eaten by bigger jellyfish. They are also eaten by sea turtles and some fish.

Jellyfish catch prey with their long, stinging tentacles. When their tentacles touch prey, **venom** is released and the prey is stunned.

The jellyfish's arms catch the prey. They pull it towards the mouth in the middle of the jellyfish.

Some kinds of jellyfish are filter feeders. They suck in seawater and prey. After they eat their prey, they release the water.

Movement

Jellyfish usually drift with the ocean **currents**. They also have a special way they can swim.

They squeeze their body together and push water out underneath. The force of the water pushes the jellyfish forward.

Jellyfish are able to swim

without using much energy.

Life Cycle

Jellyfish carry eggs on their arms. The eggs hatch into tiny creatures called planulae.

Planulae float into the water for a few days, then attach themselves to a hard surface, such as a rock. In this stage, they are called **polyps**.

Jellyfish arms do not sting like

their tentacles do.

The polyps will continue to form around each other, creating a group called a colony.

Once the colony is large enough, the polyps come together to make a tiny jellyfish called an **ephyra**.

When the jellyfish is an adult, it is called a **medusa**. Once they reach the medusa stage, they can live for up to a year.

Jellyfish Life

Jellyfish don't have a brain.

They do not communicate

with other jellyfish.

Jellyfish spend their time

drifting in the water and

eating. They can be found

alone or with other jellyfish.

Box Jellyfish

The Australian box jellyfish is one of the most dangerous jellyfish. Their venom is one of the most deadly venoms in the world.

They have tentacles that can reach ten feet long. They are also the only kind of jellyfish to have eyes.

Australian box jellyfish are found in parts of the Pacific ocean. Most are around Australia.

Population

Jellyfish populations have been growing, which can be a problem for people.

This is because of changing ocean temperatures and **overfishing**. When people overfish, jellyfish don't have as many predators.

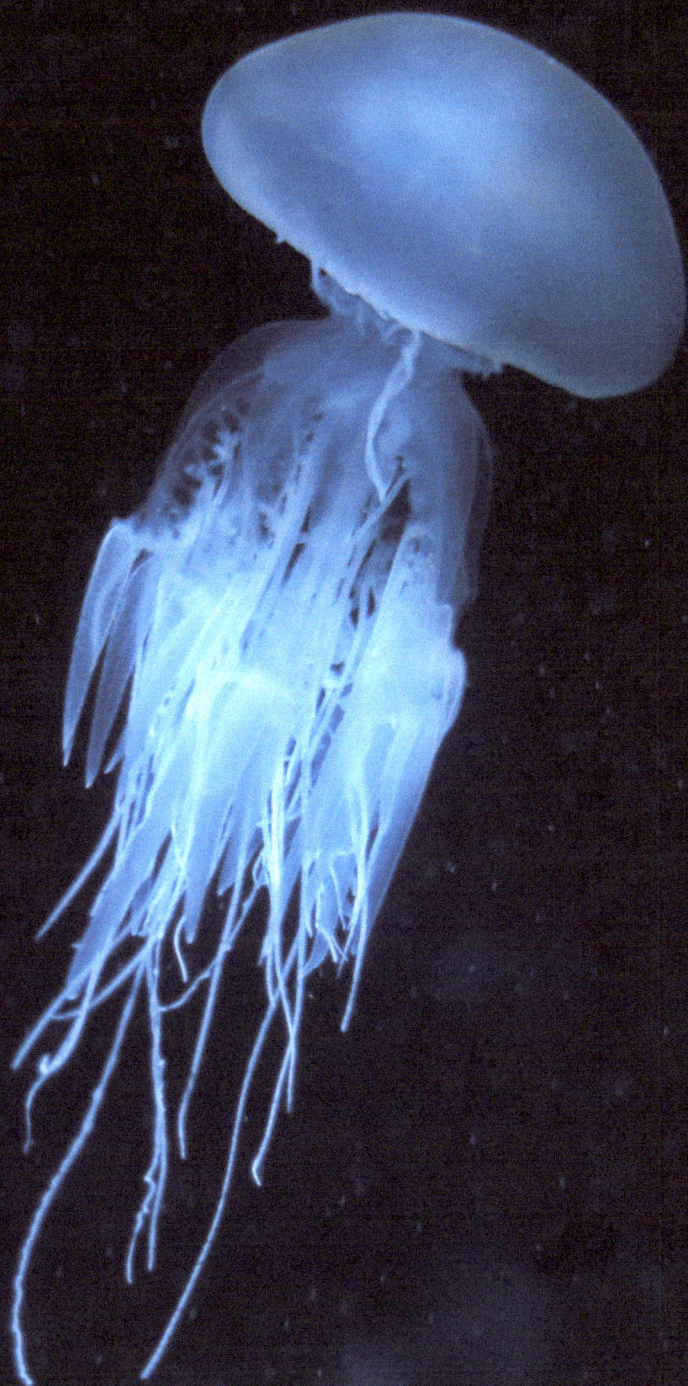

Staying Safe

If you see a jellyfish, do not touch it! Some jellyfish do not hurt humans, but some can be very dangerous.

In places where jellyfish are often found, special signs warn people to watch out for jellyfish.

MARINE
STINGERS

Most jellyfish stings will not kill humans. They are very painful. If you do get stung, rinse the area and make sure to remove the stingers.

Rinse the area with vinegar and apply baking soda. This helps to **deactivate** the stinging cells.

Jellyfish that wash up on the beach can still sting you. Watch where you are walking so you don't get stung!

Glossary

Carnivore: an animal that eats only meat

Current: the flow of the ocean

Deactivate: to stop from working, to make inactive

Ephyra: a small jellyfish that is not fully grown yet

Marine: living in the ocean

Medusa: an adult jellyfish

Overfishing: when too many fish are caught and there are population problems

Polyps: part of the jellyfish life cycle, after jellyfish hatch from eggs and attach to a surface

Structure: shape, support

Venom: poison that is made by some animals

About the Author

Victoria Blakemore is a first grade

teacher in Southwest Florida with a

passion for reading.

You can visit her at

www.elementaryexplorers.com

Also in This Series

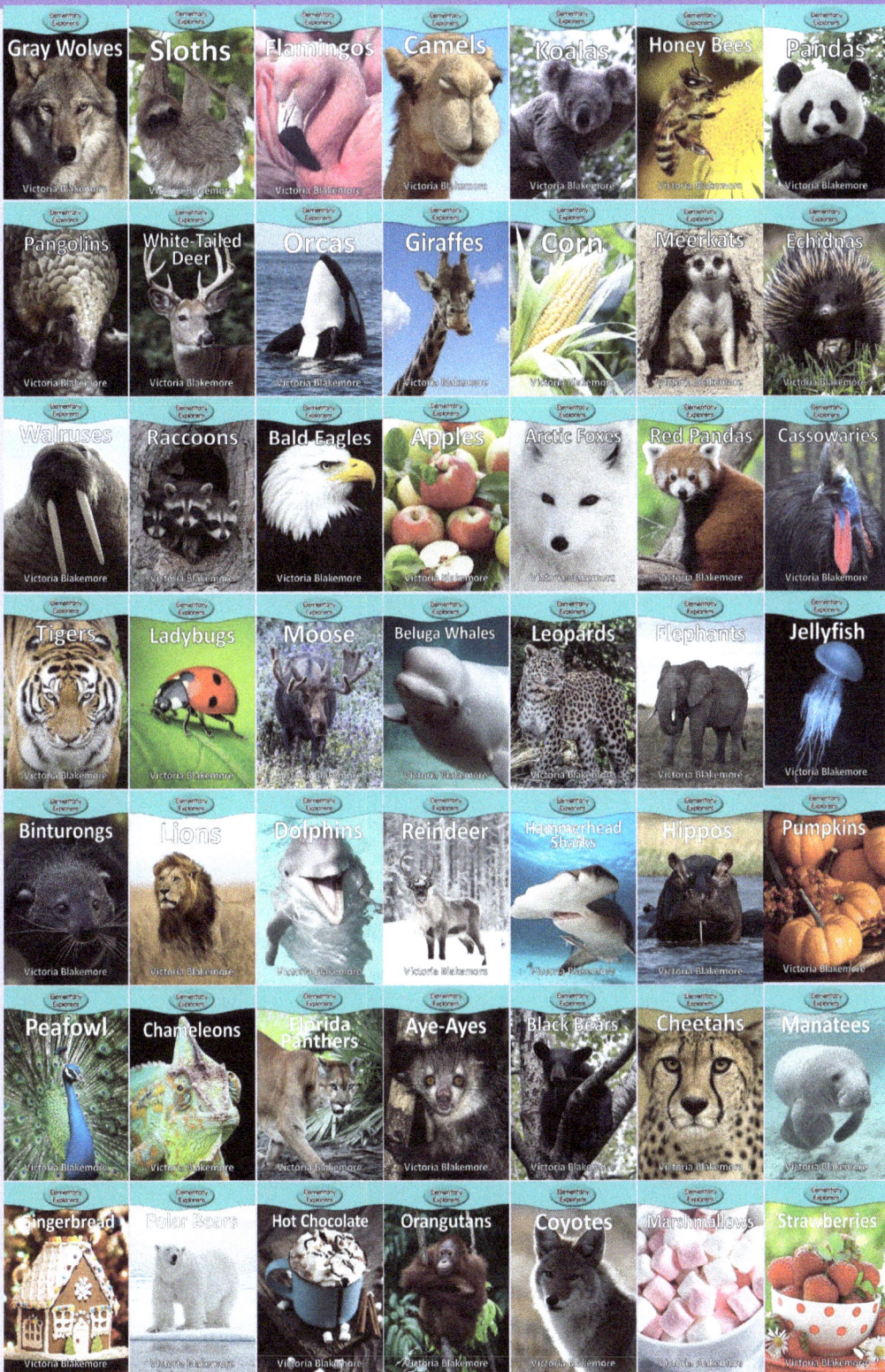

Gray Wolves	Sloths	Flamingos	Camels	Koalas	Honey Bees	Pandas
Pangolins	White-Tailed Deer	Orcas	Giraffes	Corn	Meerkats	Echidnas
Walruses	Raccoons	Bald Eagles	Apples	Arctic Foxes	Red Pandas	Cassowaries
Tigers	Ladybugs	Moose	Beluga Whales	Leopards	Elephants	Jellyfish
Binturongs	Lions	Dolphins	Reindeer	Hammerhead Sharks	Hippos	Pumpkins
Peafowl	Chameleons	Florida Panthers	Aye-Ayes	Black Bears	Cheetahs	Manatees
Gingerbread	Polar Bears	Hot Chocolate	Orangutans	Coyotes	Marshmallows	Strawberries

Victoria Blakemore

Also in This Series

Aardvarks	Mako Sharks	Alligators	Frogs	Hedgehogs	Brown Bears	Bongos
Sea Turtles	Quokkas	Muskrats	Zebras	Red Foxes	Ring-Tailed Lemurs	Platypuses
Anteaters	Kangaroos	Rhinos	Jaguars	Wombats	Capybaras	Gorillas
Cats	Skunks	Butterflies	Dingoes	Snow Leopards	African Wild Dogs	Penguins
Whale Sharks	Wolverines	Warthogs	Caracals	Badgers	Seals	Hummingbirds
Pikas	Humpback Whales	Pumas	Lemonade	Llamas	Tulips	Ostriches
Sunflowers	Fennec Foxes	Sea Lions	Squirrels	Roses	Porcupines	Ice Cream

All titles: Elementary Explorers — Victoria Blakemore

www.ingramcontent.com/pod-product-compliance
Lightning Source LLC
Chambersburg PA
CBHW051252020426
42333CB00025B/3172